EL COTILLO JO HAMMER FOTOS

COPYRIGHT JO HAMMER

www.atlantura.com

ES

El Cotillo Photos

Rodeado de cristalinas lagunas y blanca arena se encuentra un pequeño pueblo pesquero llamado El Cotillo, que hasta el día de hoy conserva su calma.solo las impresionantes olas en invierno, que en ocasiones han irrumpido en los 2 muelles, y las fiestas locales en verano interrumpen la tranquilidad. Ambas son ocasiones de gran interés turístico.

4 km al norte , pasadas las lagunas y las calas de arena, en el faro del Tostón, ya nada recuerda a la varada del Massira 1, pesquero marroquí que quedó encallado en las rocas a causa del tormentoso mar de esa noche del octubre de 1999.

Más al sur, los acantilados ofrecen una espectacular vista a la playa de 4 km, la cual disfrutan deportistas y los amantes del sol. Tras la puesta del sol el olor a pescado frito, que muy amenudo son pescados por los del pueblo, inunda las calles.

Antiguamente, El Cotillo era un pueblo que destacaba en la exportación de cal y grano a la isla de Gran Canaria. Para protegerse de los ataques de piratas construyeron la torre del Tostón, en 1741. Las piedras que la forman provienen de una cantera en las cercanías de la iglesia, la cuál fue construida en 1680 en honor a la virgen del buen viaje.

El uso del muelle ha disminuido por la difícil causada por los riscos. Ya en el año 1930 solo una pocas familias vivían de la pesca dado a que fue declarado zona turística en un intento de construir un campo de golf. El intento fracasó a causa de la presión de los ecologistas.

La crisis ha frenado el boom de la construcción y eso ha evitado que El Cotillo se convirtiese en un complejo turístico gigante. Por lo tanto, a pesar de algunas monstruosidades este pueblo mantiene su originalidad. Deseo que las futuras generaciones puedan apreciar este pequeño pueblo tal y como es ahora.

Con este libro me gustaría mostraos mis fotos, que han surgido en este peculiar pueblo.

El Cotillo. Photos

Surrounded by crystal clear lagoons and white sand there is a small fishing village called El Cotillo, which to this day retains its calm. Only the amazing waves in winter, those sometimes break into both harbors, and the local festivals in the summer break the peace. Both are times of great tourist interest.

4 km north, past the lagoons and the sandy coves at the Toston lighthouse, nothing remembers to the Stranded Massira 1, a Moroccan fishing vessel that ran aground on the rocks because of the stormy sea one night tide of October 1999.

Further south, the cliffs offer a spectacular view of the beach of 4 km, which enjoy sport fanatics and sun lovers. After sunset the smell of fried fish which is caught by the local people, floods the streets.

Formerly, El Cotillo was a town that formed part of the export of lime and grain to the island of Gran Canaria. To protect against pirate attacks, the Toston tower was built in 1741. Stones that came form from a nearby quarry where used to built the church in 1680 in honor of the Virgin of good travel (Virgen del buen viaje).

The use of the harbor has decreased because of the difficult cliffs. Already in 1930 just a few families lived from fishing because it was declared tourist area in an attempt to build a golf course. The attempt failed because of pressure from environmentalists.

The recesion has slowed the construction boom and this has prevented that El Cotillo becomes a giant resort. Therefore, despite some monstrosities this town maintains its originality.

I wish that future generations can appreciate this small town as it is now.

With this book I would like to show you some of my photos, which have emerged in this peculiar place.

DE

El Cotillo Fotos

Von grünen Lagunen und weißen Sandstränden umgeben, hat sich das kleine Fischerdorf El Cotillo bis heute seine ursprüngliche Ruhe bewahrt. Im Winter sorgen nur die gigantische Atlantikwellen, die sich vor den beiden Häfen auftürmen für Unruhe. Das Ende August stattfindende Dorffest, und „Fuerteventura en musica", ein zwei tägiges Open Air Konzert an der Playa de la concha im Juni, ziehen jedes Jahr mehr Touristen und Einheimische in ihren Bann. Vier Kilometer nördlich von El Cotillo, vorbei an Lagunen und Sandbuchten beim Leuchtturm „El Toston", erinnert nichts mehr an die Strandung des 30 Meter langen marokkanischen Fischkutters „Massira 1". Das Schiff wurde in einer Oktobernacht 1999 von einer mörderischen Brandung auf die Felsen geworfen. Im Süden bietet die Steilküste einen idealen Blick auf den vier Kilometer langen Strand, an dem sich Wassersportler und Sonnenhungrige tummeln. Nach dem Sonnenuntergang zieht der Duft von gebratenem Fisch durch die Gassen, der in den Restaurants noch direkt von den einheimischen Fischern kommt. El Cotillo war einmal ein bedeutender Hafen von dem Getreide und gebrannter Kalk nach Gran Canaria verschifft wurde. Aus Schutz vor Piratenüberfällen wurde 1741 der Festungsturm „Torre de Toston" erbaut. Die Steine stammen aus einem Steinbruch in der Nähe der 1680 erbauten Kirche „La Ermita del Toston", die der „Virgen del Buen Viaje" (Jungfrau der guten Reise) gewidmet ist. Um 1930 lebten in El Cotillo nur noch wenige Familien vom Fischfang. Der alte Hafen ist wegen vorgelagerter Riffs und der schwierigen Hafeneinfahrt immer weniger benutzt worden. Seit der Ort vor einigen Jahren von der Regierung zur touristischen Zone erklärt wurde, ist der Versuch, hier einen großflächigen Golfplatz anzulegen, an dem massiven Druck von Umweltverbänden und Naturschützern gescheitert. Auch das Überbauen des kleinen Fischerdorfs mit touristischen Großkomplexen, ist dank der Finanzkriese vorerst gestoppt. Trotz einiger Bausünden hat sich El Cotillo viel von dem ursprünglichen Scharm eines kanarischen Fischerdorfes erhalten. Es ist wünschenswert das sich in Zukunft noch viele Generationen an der einmaligen Natur dieser Zone erfreuen können.

Mit diesem Fotoband möchte ich eine Auswahl meiner Fotos, die im Laufe der Jahre in und um El Cotillo entstanden sind präsentieren.

El Cotillo

Puerto nuevo

Puerto nuevo y el Muellito

El Muellito

Caleta del Cotillo

Playa de Marfolin

Roca de la mar

Castillo de Rico Roque

Castillo de Rico Roque

Pescador de El Cotillo

Roca del mar

Playa del Castillo

El Muellito

Roca del mar

Faro del Toston

Faro del Toston

Caleta de la Aduana

Castillo de Rico Roque

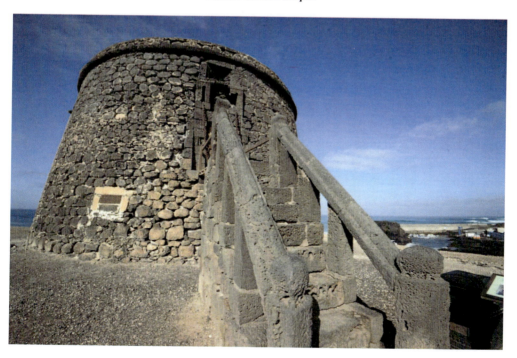

Castillo de Rico Roque

El Muellito

Rico Roque del mar

Puerto nuevo

Puerto nuevo

Puerto nuevo

Puerto nuevo

Olas en la costa del El Cotillo

Puerto nuevo

Puerto nuevo

Castillo de Rico Roque

Castillo de Rico Roque

Grandes Playas

El Muellito

El Muellito

El Cotillo

El Muellito

Massira I

Massira I

Massira I

Massira I

El Muellito

El Muellito

El Muellito

El Muellito

El Muellito

Castillo de Rico Roque

Playa de Aguila

Playa de Aguila

Playa de Castillo

Charco de Guelde

Playa Esquinzo

Playa Esquinzo

Piedra Playa

Fiesta en El Cotillo

Fiesta en El Cotillo

Fiesta en honor Ntra Sra del Buen Viaje

Fiesta en honor Ntra Sra del Buen Viaje

Ntra Sra del Buen Viaje

Fiesta en El Cotillo

Fiesta del agua

Salema

Salema

Playa de Marfolin

Playa de la concha

Playas de los lagos

Playa de Marfolin

Playa de la concha

Rincon de los Morteros

La Costilla

La Marisma

Playa del Marfolin

Los Lagos

Playa de la Concha

El Banadero

El Cotillo

El Cotillo

El Muellito

El Muellito

Calera

Roca de la mar

Playa de Marfolin

Playa de la concha

Punta Mallorquín

Playa del Castillo

Nubes de la manana en El Cotillo

Herstellung und Verlag:
BoD - Books on Demand, Norderstedt
ISBN 978-3-7357-5950-4

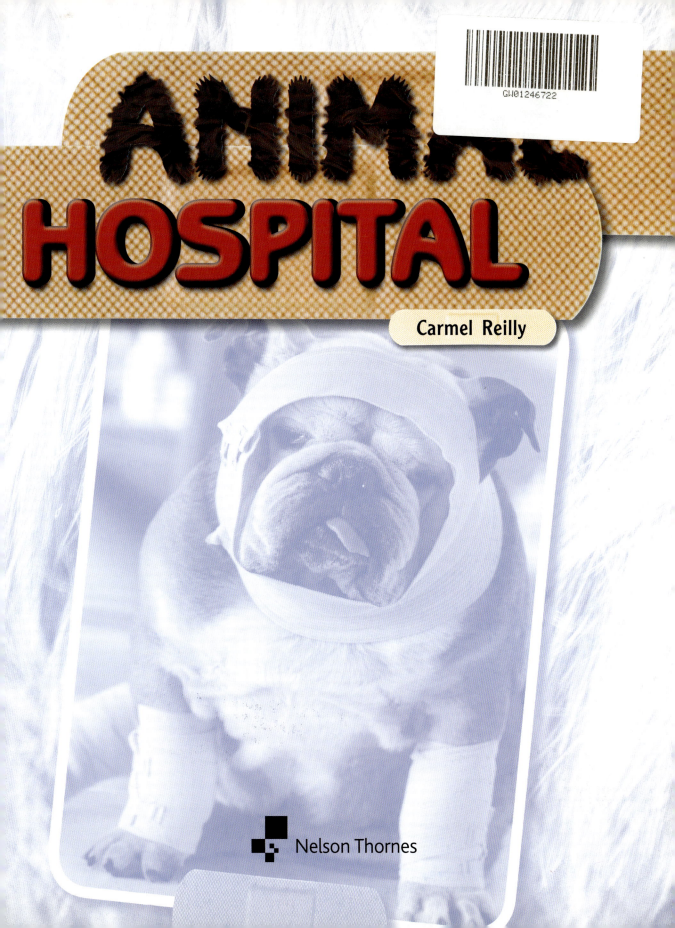
ANIMAL HOSPITAL

Carmel Reilly

Nelson Thornes

First published in 2007 by Cengage Learning Australia
www.cengage.com.au

This edition published in 2008 under the imprint of Nelson Thornes Ltd,
Delta Place, 27 Bath Road, Cheltenham, United Kingdom, GL53 7TH

10 9 8 7 6 5 4 3 2
11 10 09 08

Text © 2007 Cengage Learning Australia Pty Ltd ABN 14058280149
(incorporated in Victoria)

The right of Carmel Reilly to be identified as author of this work has been asserted by him/her in accordance with the Copyright, Designs and Patents Act 1988

All rights reserved. No part of this publication may be reproduced or transmitted in any form or by any means, electronic or mechanical, including photocopy, recording or any information storage and retrieval system, without permission in writing from the publisher or under licence from the Copyright Licensing Agency Limited, of 90 Tottenham Court Road, London W1T 4LP.

Any person who commits any unauthorised act in relation to this publication may be liable to criminal prosecution and civil claims for damages.

Animal Hospital
ISBN 978-1-4085-0083-5

Text by Carmel Reilly
Edited by Johanna Rohan
Designed by Vonda Pestana
Series Design by James Lowe
Production Controller Hanako Smith
Photo Research by Corrina Tauschke
Audio recordings by Juliet Hill, Picture Start
Spoken by Matthew King and Abbe Holmes
Printed in China by 1010 Printing International Ltd

Website www.nelsonthornes.com

Acknowledgements
The author and publisher would like to acknowledge permission to reproduce material from the following sources:
Photographs by Alamy/Jack Sullivan, p. 10; APL/Corbis/LWA-Dann Tardif, cover, pp. 1, 11 left, 13; Fairfaxphotos/Paul Harris, p. 14; Getty Images/Skip Nall, p. 8/ Arthur Tilley, p. 6; Newsphotos.com/Peter Clark, p. 10 inset/ Daniel Griffiths, p. 4 right/ Dale Mann, p. 4 left/ Kris Reichl, p. 15; Photolibrary.com/ Superstock, Inc, p. 12/ Photolibrary.com/Animals Animals/Sanchez, Juan M. & De Lope L., p. 7 inset/ Stockdale, Renee, pp. 3, 11 right/ Weimann, Peter, p. 7; REUTERS/Debra Sally/Picture Media, p. 9.

ANIMAL HOSPITAL

Carmel Reilly

Contents

Chapter 1	**Starting the Day**	4
Chapter 2	**The Vet Arrives**	8
Chapter 3	**The Animals Arrive**	10
Glossary and Index		16

Chapter 1

STARTING THE DAY

An animal hospital is a place for sick or hurt animals.
Sick or hurt animals go to **intensive care** when they first arrive at the animal hospital.

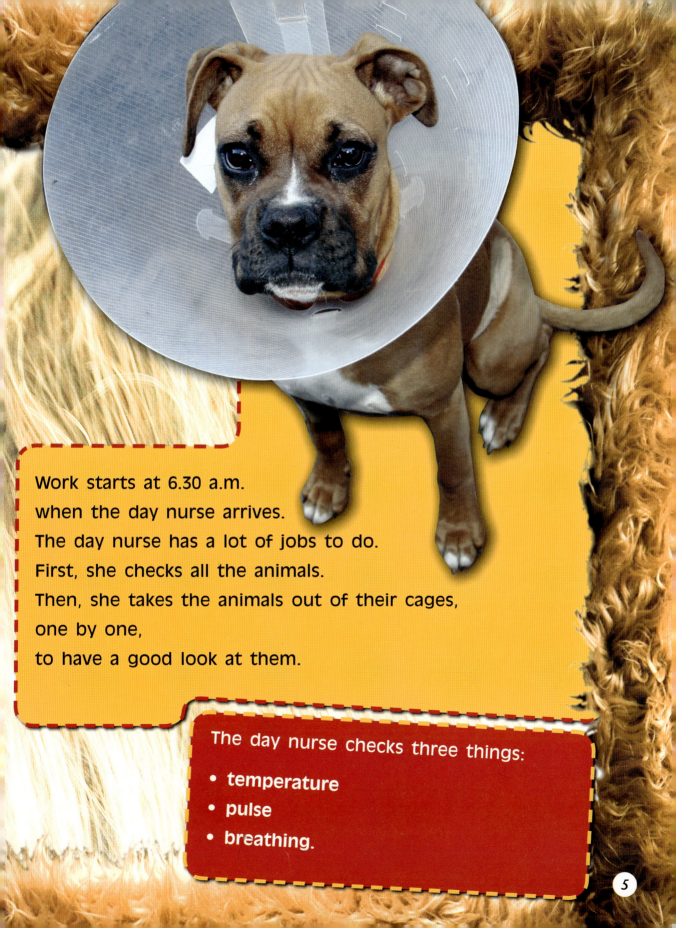

Work starts at 6.30 a.m.
when the day nurse arrives.
The day nurse has a lot of jobs to do.
First, she checks all the animals.
Then, she takes the animals out of their cages,
one by one,
to have a good look at them.

The day nurse checks three things:
- **temperature**
- **pulse**
- **breathing.**

The day nurse also checks to see if the animals look happy, and if they are eating well.

Then, the day nurse gives the animals their medicine and cleans their cages.

THE VET ARRIVES

At 8.00 a.m., the vet arrives at the animal hospital.
The vet goes to intensive care first to see how the animals are.
After she has looked at them,
she thinks about what to do with them next.

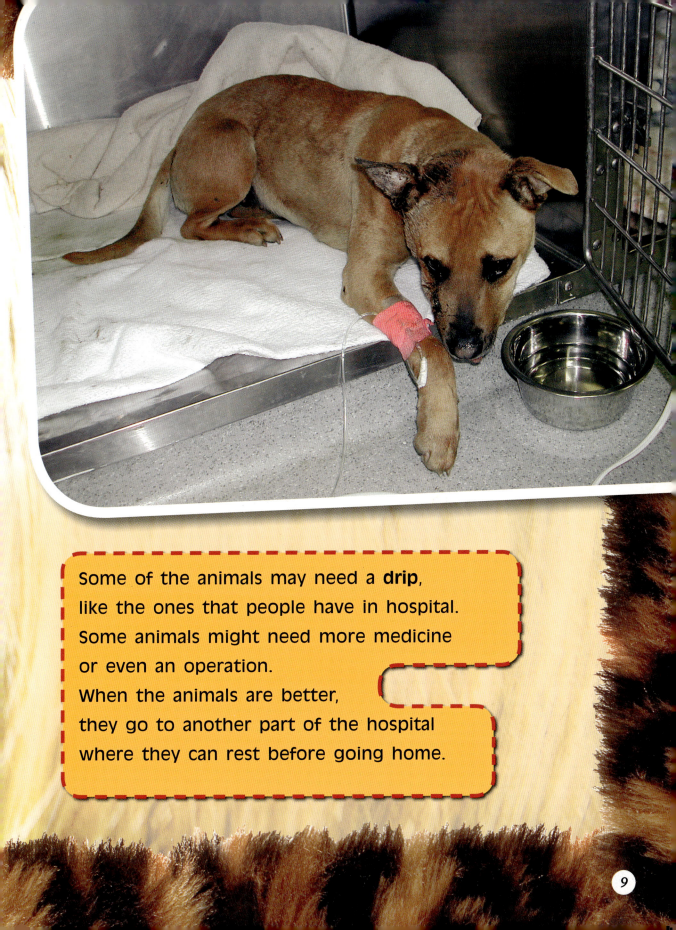

Some of the animals may need a **drip**, like the ones that people have in hospital. Some animals might need more medicine or even an operation.
When the animals are better, they go to another part of the hospital where they can rest before going home.

THE ANIMALS ARRIVE

New animals arrive at the animal hospital all the time.

Sometimes, they have been hit by a car or hurt by another animal.
Sometimes, they have been eating something that is not good for them, like poison.

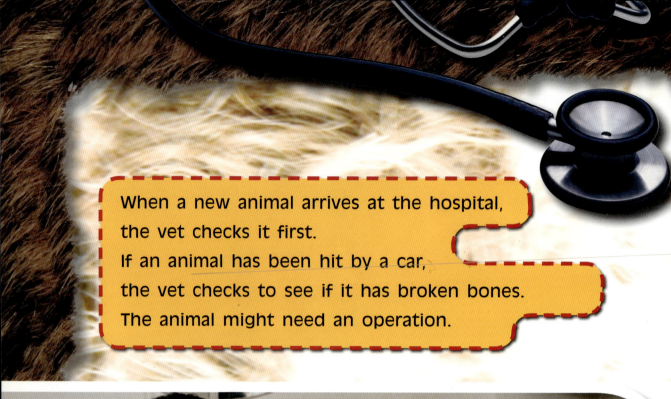

When a new animal arrives at the hospital, the vet checks it first.
If an animal has been hit by a car, the vet checks to see if it has broken bones.
The animal might need an operation.

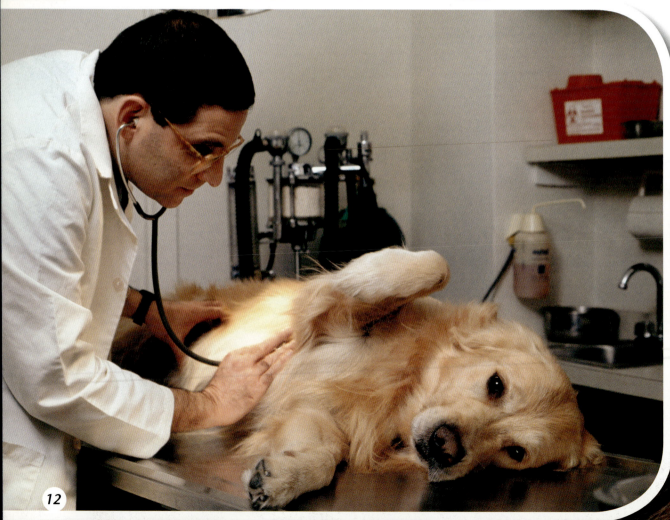

After this, the animal goes to intensive care, where it is looked after by the nurse.

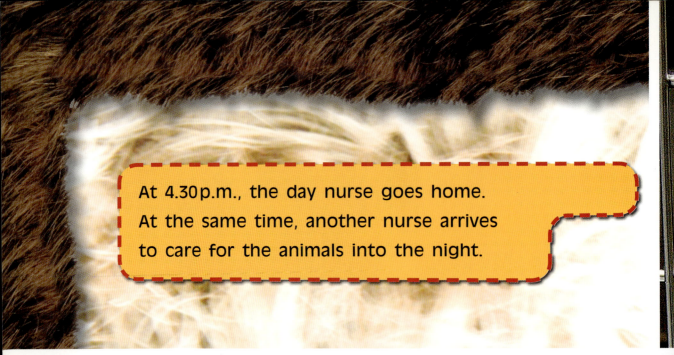

At 4.30 p.m., the day nurse goes home. At the same time, another nurse arrives to care for the animals into the night.

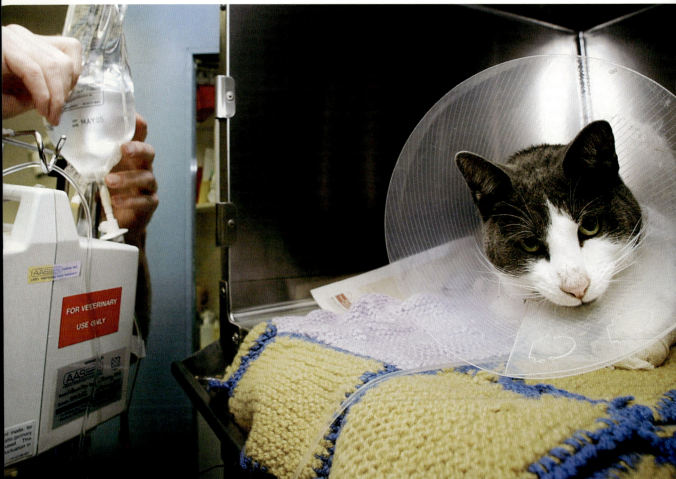

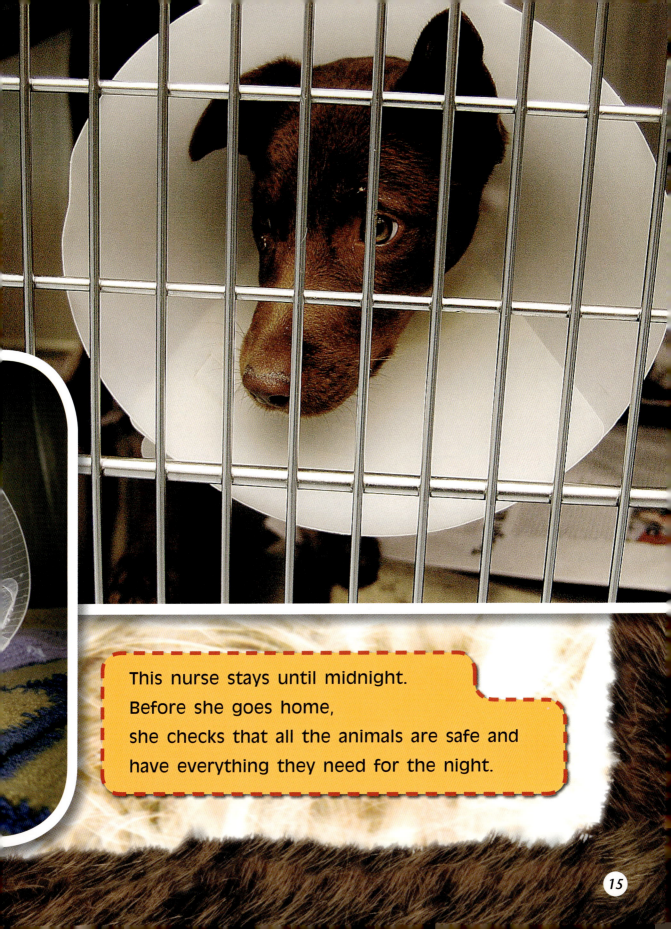

This nurse stays until midnight.
Before she goes home,
she checks that all the animals are safe and have everything they need for the night.

Glossary

breathing to take air into the lungs. A sick animal may not be breathing well.

drip medicine that goes into a sick animal's blood

intensive care the animals that are in this part of the hospital get a lot of special care because they have been badly hurt or are very ill

pulse an animal's pulse shows how fast its heart is beating

temperature how hot or cold an animal is

Index

breathing 5
broken bones 12
cages 5, 7
drip 9
intensive care 4, 8, 13
medicine 7, 9

nurse 5, 6, 7, 13, 14–15
operation 9, 12
poison 11
pulse 5
temperature 5
vet 8, 12